WHY VOLUNTEERS GET ALL THE BREAKS

Eric B. Barnes

iUniverse, Inc.

New York   Bloomington

iUniverse books may be ordered through booksellers or by contacting:

iUniverse
1663 Liberty Drive
Bloomington, IN 47403
www.iuniverse.com
1-800-Authors (1-800-288-4677)

ISBN: 978-1-4401-4474-5 (sc)
ISBN: 978-1-4401-4475-2 (ebook)

Printed in the United States of America

iUniverse rev. date: 06/02/2009

Table of Contents

Prologue: When Is It Finally Gonna Be Your Break Time?

When I first thought of writing this book, I knew immediately what direction I wanted to go with it. I knew I wanted to advise people – particularly unemployed people and people who are struggling to find their vocation in life – to consider volunteering as critical strategy for the journey. But when I actually started putting the wheels in motion, must admit I had doubts about where I was going.

For a short while, I started thinking, "Wait a minute. Isn't volunteering is something generous people do graciously with their time?" I proceeded to think, "Well, won't my book encourage people to be just the opposite? Won't my book encourage people to be selfish, to use volunteering merely as a means to an end?" I kept on writing, but this thought popped up every now and then and kept nagging me.

But as the internal naggings continued, they eventually provoked some thought and insight. I suddenly remembered how I started as a volunteer. The more I thought about my earliest days as a volunteer, the more I realized that my motives were not exactly of the most selfless variety. In fact, volunteering wasn't even my idea. I had never even thought about it.

There I was, months and months drowned deeply into unemployment. The gap in time between the present and the time the last bit of my work experience ended was getting bigger and more noticeable with each passing month. Lucky for me, during a casual conversation with my aunt one day about my increasingly desperate unemployment situation, she suggested that I do some volunteer work just to keep that hole in my resume from getting any bigger. She told me I should do volunteer work just so I can say in my next job interview that I was doing something. Her suggestion sounded good to me because I was really starting to sense employers were not impressed with my "I've been job-*hunting*" notion.

So there I was. I became a volunteer. But to help others selflessly? No, not really. (What? Would you rather I lie to you?) I became a volunteer because I needed something new to put on my resume. My resume looked like I hadn't done shit for eight months! I wasn't trying to be good, I was trying to be employed.

But the richness of the experience grabbed a hold of me. After a couple of months of steady volunteering, I realized that I was helping people and making a difference. Soon I realized I was enjoying just being part of the experience.

Next thing I knew, three or four months into volunteering at the hospital, people started asking me when was I going to apply to work full-time. I didn't apply at that time because I had another part-time job aside from the volunteering. But I soon realized that the best part of my week (at least as far as work was concerned) was the three to four hours I was volunteering at the hospital. So I celebrated my eight-month anniversary with an application. The rest was history.

My point in bringing this up is there is so much that can be gained if more people would consider volunteering as part of their job search. Sure, most people probably won't have the right motives going in (if there are any "right" motives). But sometimes you have to go to a place to find out why you need to be there. I believe volunteering will make many people's job prospecting far easier. And as a bonus, customer service in our society stands to drastically improve if more people learned it through the volunteering experience.

Personally, I can't see how you can turn down what I'm offering in this book. I'm offering you the chance to participate in what is among the most selfless acts in the world – volunteering – and do something selfish with it. Namely finding, gaining, and developing contacts for *your*self, *your* benefit. To take something noble and use it for your benefit.

Take a few moments to consider what you stand to gain by volunteering, and then stop thinking and start working!

Introduction

What does it mean to claim that volunteers get all the breaks? Well, that is precisely the question I intend to address and hopefully answer in this book.

How many times have you said to yourself, "If only someone would hire me, I would prove myself worthy?" How many times have you been certain that your new business venture would be a great service to the community if only people would give it a chance?

The bad economic times we have endured recently have multiplied the usual hardships that accompany our attempts to gain employment or to start our own businesses. There is so much advice available from so many well-intentioned sources as to how to get us moving to acquiring employment and ultimately success for ourselves. Unfortunately far too much advice has been too long recycled, and suffering from a lack of innovation and creativity. As much as we all appreciate learning how to become better marketers of ourselves, when the well that is your finances is drying up daily, you need income, and you need it now.

Volunteering no longer just for the few, the noble, the people who supposedly have extra time to spare. Volunteering may be the best, and in some cases the only way to get a job in an economy where the hiring to firing ratio is grossly disproportionate. Now more than ever employing establishments are hiring who they know first.

If you have not learned anything else from our sagged economy, hopefully you learned that Plan A, B, & C are not good enough anymore. You need to have Plans A through Z ready to go into motion should the time come to put any of them to work. And if volunteering somewhere is not part of your plans, your plans are not complete.

This book aims to encourage you to consider volunteering your products and services as a way to convince others to try out what you have to offer. Whether you are trying to get a job, start a career, or start a business, you are not getting anywhere if you cannot gain the interests of employers of your services or consumers of your products. My goal is to convince you that by allowing others to sample what you have to offer for free, they may be more willing to give you a chance to prove yourself. I have no doubt that a lot of struggling people in this world could really become a big hit if only they could "get in the door" to prove themselves.

Throughout this book, I will refer to those for whom you'd be volunteering as *employers*, the reason being that you could potentially volunteer for many types of establishments. You could volunteer for a club, an organization, an institution, a government, even a corporation. Another reason I will refer to them as employers is because this book aims to point you toward seeking volunteering opportunities for establishments with employees (as opposed to, say, volunteering to mow your neighbor's grass for free). The point of this book is to help you turn volunteering into a source of opportunity in order to bring increased success into your life, not to teach you how to be a noble individual. Of course, I definitely hope volunteering does give you "that good feeling inside" of knowing you helped some folks out and asked for nothing in return. But the real purpose is to give someone a reason, and a motivation, to pay for your products or services.

For this to work, you will need to learn (or rediscover) the virtue of patience. The path of the volunteer will not reap rewards overnight. I strongly encourage you to start a plan and work that plan throughout your volunteering experience. For our purposes, your experience is not complete without your exercising a healthy curiosity. While volunteering, you should be meeting people, asking questions, learning about the employer, and discovering job opportunities within.

Volunteering for Success

A vast array of possibilities and opportunities come with being a volunteer. There is the constant opportunity to learn and grow, advance yourself, develop contacts, discover a new field of endeavor, and meet interesting people, especially people who could become future employers, customers, or business associates. If you have not even considered becoming a volunteer, then you are ignoring a path that can conceivably make a huge difference in your life. You give so little as a volunteer compared to what you potentially get in return. Sometimes volunteering can put you in the right place at the right time.

You can develop new skills while meeting new people while lending a hand to someone in need. Some people simply cannot seem to get past the idea or concept of volunteering as a way to work for someone for free, for no money, for nothing in return. But just because you are not paid money, that does not mean you are not paid. One attitude problem in our country is the constant need for immediate compensation. Far too few people are willing to take the long-term view, and pay their dues while delaying momentary reward. Little wonder those with the patience see such huge reward later on. Volunteers do not get a paycheck, but they get something far more valuable. Volunteers get something that won't run out every week, or every other week.

Those who volunteer for success bring their time, attention, and energy to their daily tasks. But more important, volunteers for success bring their dreams, their vision, to their daily tasks. No, volunteers do not work all day everyday like employees. But they do dream big everyday. You see, when people dream big and carry a huge vision of success in their minds at all times, no task is too big or too small or too daunting for them. People who enable themselves to see the greatness of tomorrow's success have the patience and fortitude to forgo nibbling on today's scraps in favor of diving into tomorrow's feast.

Add all that to the fact that even now, while volunteers are not getting paid (well, at least not money), they get perks, opportunities, and a big boatload of thanks. People rarely forget to appreciate volunteers because they are there to help out although they don't have to be there.

When you offer your products and services for free, you give people more than just your promotional drivel as the reason they should invest their money in you. Because job candidates are basically selling themselves to get a job, it's fair to say they have (or should have) a marketing plan. Their tools include resumes, cover letters, and thank-you notes. Their strategies include interviews, follow-up calls, and sessions. So often when you go to a job interview, you are trying to convince a stranger, someone who knows almost or completely nothing about you, to do long-term investing in you. Your resume, cover letter, interviews, and what not have to convince this company of strangers how it would serve their best interests to hire you over dozens and even hundreds of other strangers, many of whom have similar qualifications and are likely making the same claims you are. How do you set yourself apart? Remember, whomever any employer hires will be someone they believe will contribute greatly to increased profits and better reputation, as well as make them more competitive in the marketplace. And yes, that even includes custodial, maintenance, clerical and other less prestigious positions.

No Time To Wait

Most of us are aware that who you know will trump what you know any ol' day of the week. But the further the economy sinks into hell, who you know becomes even more important than usual. Volunteer. Get involved. Be part of something. But get busy now. No time to wait until later.

If you get busy volunteering now, while you are freshly unemployed, you may never have a chance to become desperately unemployed. And for those who have already started swimming in unemployment, get busy volunteering now, and take the first step toward turning that situation around.

The idea of volunteering may seem silly to you now, but when you wake up one day and realize you have four or five months of volunteering behind you, you may discover that unlike those in a similar situation, you've done something to help remedy your situation. Take any two people who have been unemployed for, say, six months. Both of them have been improving their resumes, fine tuning their cover letters, and even being fortunate enough to be called in for that occasional interview. Except only one of them has spent the last six months volunteering. The one who has been volunteering for the past six months is miles ahead of the other because the volunteer has far more contacts, connections, resources, and experience and his/her immediate disposal than the other.

But the two people mentioned above represent something else: the difference between someone waiting for a miracle and someone making a miracle happen. As you ponder all the possible reasons you constantly come so close to getting that new job, but never quite make it all the way to the finish line, I want you to reflect upon your actions (or lack thereof) lately. It is entirely possible that no one is hiring you because you do not appeal to them as an action-oriented person who gets results, who gets things done. You do not seem resourceful. You seem to them to be the kind of person who waits for things to happen. Who puts your destiny in other people's hands. Who waits for other people to act before you will.

Demonstrate determination to employers, and they will see they stand to lose much by rejecting you. If you volunteer, your determination is on display. You're not waiting for someone to give you a chance, you are giving yourself a chance. There's no time to wait to get started. There is no wait until tomorrow. Tomorrow will have its own troubles and struggles and, I might add, source of excuses. Tomorrow sucks. Start today!

Stop Prospecting and Get To Work!

You have several choices. You can read newspaper articles that teach you how to spice up your resume or add little dazzle to your cover letter or how to be a better, more effective job interviewee. You can work with a career counselor who can help give you that edge over your competition. You can spend hours upon days upon weeks upon months working on your job interviewing skills, learning etiquette for various job interview settings, and discovering the right words to say at the right times to make yourself the preferred candidate. You can even learn all the nonverbal communication mechanics of job interviewing, such as how to handle your nonverbals and how to interpret the interviewer's. All of the above is a huge waste of time.

What you need to understand is that more often than not you are either the right candidate or you're not. It's admirable of you to suppose there is a lot of gray in this area, but things may be more black and white than you realize. Candidates get so disappointed when they believe they did everything right at the job interview, the interviewer tells them something that practically confirms this belief, and they still get rejected. What these job candidates probably did not realize is that most likely they were rejected in favor of someone the employer knew better. Perhaps if you are willing to broaden the scope of your vision, you can get busy doing volunteer work for someone between resume and interview improvement sessions with your career counselors. You should never allow another 168-hour week of unemployment to pass without devoting at least four of those hours to volunteer work. Volunteering is not just about the work. Volunteering is about the people you meet, the connections you make, the skills you learn, the discovery you gain of yourself.

It really makes me grin to hear out-of-work people saying they don't have time to volunteer. Oh well, I guess it can be pretty busy to have too much time on your hands. This all stems from the narrow-minded laziness that is so prevalent in our culture. So many people don't want to do anything unless they are going to get paid, in advance, at a higher than average salary, for the least amount of work possible. With a possible handful of exceptions, that's just not reality. And even the majority of those exceptions are not going to happen unless you have lavish connections that know you already, and know you damn well!

Every day that you waste not making new connections could possibly be worth up to a month of lost job opportunities. You could be volunteering for your future employer, or you could meet someone at the volunteer assignment that can give you what you need to move forward. It is so amazing what a difference can be made in our lives because we were at the right place at the right time. Volunteering can put you there. Don't you think it's about time you are the candidate being hired over everyone else not because you are the most qualified, but because you are the one who knew the right people?

Volunteering Versus Job Interviewing

Boy, oh boy…..job interviews. Aren't they a treat? Allow me to offer you a piece of advice that's worth more than ten job offers: stop interviewing so much. One day you're going to find you are still unemployed, but hey, you sure can conduct yourself in a job interview! Being a master interviewee is not being employed. Many people I know, including myself, have been rejected by potential employers *after* being told we were damn fine interviewees (although not in those exact words). Volunteer somewhere, and replace talk with action. Start doing something someone can see and appreciate, and stop sitting in someone's office yapping claims of how you'd be the best thing that ever happened to the employer. Besides, it doesn't matter how good or qualified you are or claim to be. There is still a better than average chance you will be rejected in favor of someone the employer knows better, regardless of how much that person's attributes fall short of yours in comparison. Never forget the real goal, which is not to be the best interviewee, but to get the job. Besides, you will never be the best until you are given an opportunity to prove you are the best.

Right or wrong, fair or cruel, good economy or bad economy, the big breaks will always be more readily available to those who have the most promising connections. While people are beating themselves up supposing they didn't get the job because they screwed up the interview or didn't have enough education or experience, or even that bullshit about not being "the right fit", their real nemesis was more likely someone more previously, and/or personally, acquainted with the employer.

Why don't you give yourself an unfair advantage for a change? Haven't you spent more than enough time studying a bunch of skills and strategies and techniques for successful job interviewing? I'm advising you to give a little of your time and energy to something that can provide for you the knowledge, skills, connections, and that invaluable "inside look" that you cannot beat with a stick! Trust me, if you give someone three to four hours of your week for volunteer work, you'll still have 35-plus hours to waste perfecting your resume and interviewing techniques.

Personally, I'll take volunteering over job interviewing any day of the week. Job interviewing consists heavily of two of my biggest pet peeves: describing myself and kissing ass.

Resume Building Versus Resume Tweaking

In life, there are problem finders and there are problem solvers. Opening your mind opens the door to a variety of solutions to any problem. One of the reasons many people who are out of work stay out of work is because they have found the problem – unemployment – and they have found the one solution – job interviews, and as many as possible. But if you really open your mind and take a look at your unemployment problem, you can easily find that there are better, easier, and more effective remedies to your unemployment problem than improving your resume, improving your cover letter, learning interviewing techniques, and all that other job-finding crap.

Unlike job interviewing, volunteering is not just one option. Volunteering is a variety of options, in and of itself. While others are on their laptops and PCs, or in computer labs and Internet cafes tweaking their resumes, volunteers are building their resumes. And building experience will always prove more useful than preparing ass-kissing material.

People who lose in life will always find someone to blame for their loss. But creative people will be too busy finding other solutions to remedy their loss. You will never have enough time and energy for both excuses and solutions. Sooner or later, you're going to have to decide which you will spend more of your time and energy with. Before you decide, remember both excuses and solutions are expensive. But only one will give you your effort's worth.

If you are on your sixth month of unemployment, what the hell have you been doing for the past five months? Imagine this: as soon as you became unemployed, you started doing volunteer work. Worst case scenario, you'd be on your sixth month as a volunteer, but still unemployed. Yet you would have six months of experience to add to the experience you gained before you became unemployed. No doubt you'd have picked up at least a couple of job skills, but more likely a dozen or so. In addition, you'd have met countless people, gotten an inside look on the workings of the establishment (or several establishments for you more ambitious types), and have six months of contacts, connections, and resources that you did not have before. All of this is at your disposal; all of this can get to work helping you to land solid employment. And you'd very likely be a better person, certainly a more promising job candidate, because of it all. Tell me now that wasn't six months well spent!

Back to reality, perhaps you haven't started making the six months described above happen. Well, get started now. You've already wasted too much time, pulling yourself no closer to opportunity. Do not allow another day to go by without getting started on volunteer work. The only thing worse than regretting not having done in the past is still not doing in the present.

My point is it's time to stop being a victim. The state of the economy will get better and get worse, employers will decide to hire you and fire you, opportunities will be available and absent. Is the quality of your life always going to be dictated by which direction all the forces of the world decide to travel? I hope not, my friend, because I sure would not want outside forces deciding how I live my life.

Volunteering is a chance to take back control of your life. Because when you are a volunteer, you decide. There are so many opportunities out there, in all different fields, just waiting for someone to grab. There is no reason anybody should feel stuck in a job they hate. Or why anyone should feel the only way to do what they would love to do for a living requires them to enroll in an expensive educational institution program that will drive them deeper into debt without the balance of opportunity on the other side of the scale.

Where Should I Volunteer?

As much as I'd like to advise you to take some time to reflect upon what area you would fit best as a volunteer, the fact is if you have been out of work for some time already, you've wasted more than enough time thinking as it is. Now is the time for action. It's time to find something interesting and get to work volunteering and making connections right now. You can decide later where you'd fit best. If you have rarely or never volunteered before, chances are you have little to no idea of the vast opportunities available to put your skills and interests to work through volunteering. And let's not forget, you may have skills, talents, and interests that you haven't even discovered yet!

Time is of the essence. Every month you remain unemployed and doing nothing constructive, the gap in your resume is getting bigger. Allow me to take some of the pressure of figuring out where to volunteer away from you. Below is a generic list of establishments in your city or town where you may find a variety of volunteering opportunities:

animal shelter	zoo
park district	hospital
school district	international volunteer organization
theatre	religious organization
homeless shelter	youth center
nursing home	political activist group

social services organization	educational institution
legal aid	conservatory
animal rights organization	planetarium
aquarium	crisis intervention hotline
museum	rehabilitation center

And I have not even hit the tip of the iceberg! There is no interest for which there is no volunteer opportunity. You can visit http://www.volunteermatch.org/, or you can browse the yellow pages. Or you can go to your favorite search engine and type in the name of your city or town and one the words above, or the word "volunteering." For example, you can Google search "Volunteering in Chicago" or Yahoo! search "Chicago homeless shelters."

Finding a place to put your volunteering interests to work is no problem at all. The problem is finding your willingness to give volunteering a try.

Find Opportunity Swiftly

There are many breeds of volunteer establishments. Some volunteer positions require formalities such as interviewing, paperwork, and background checks. Other volunteering positions just require you to show up, meet the people in charge, and get to work. If you don't like the processes that one place makes you go through to volunteer there, go somewhere else. This is not anything you need to give yourself a migraine over.

Let me make a suggestion. If you are unemployed and applying for one of those volunteering positions that have a month-long process to get you started, keep the process going, but also volunteer somewhere else that will let you start more immediately while you are waiting. Besides, another volunteering position will open the door to another experience with another bunch of potential contacts and so forth. But don't sit around waiting. There are employers who have a process that volunteers must go through every bit as much as full time employees do. The process (i.e., applications, background checks, references) may be that employer's preference, or it may be required by law.

Plenty of volunteering spots are flexible. Many not only allow, but encourage, volunteers to move from one position to another from time to time. Just remember, the employer is glad to have your help, regardless of what function you provide that help in. Sure, there are positions that need volunteers more urgently than others, but the establishment will likely want to place you where you are happiest and most comfortable. But they need you to express interest in what you want. Volunteers with healthy curiosities will gain a fuller, more rewarding experience than volunteers who just go with the flow.

Value of Volunteering

Connections. You've gotta have connections, don't you? Or do you disagree with that old saying "It's not *what* you know, it's *who* you know?" Nowadays we have so many references at our disposal. Never before has it been so easy or convenient to go back to school to get that advanced degree. Career counselors come in all shapes and sizes, from the friend who always seems to know what's in demand to the school counselor to the professional who will guide you for a small fee. Resume, cover letter, and other "marketing yourself" advice is found everywhere from the career day handout to the Sunday newspaper to cyberspace. Networking events are abounded in just about every field imaginable. Yet somehow, the old fashioned inside game is still the easiest, fastest, smoothest, and arguably best way to get in the door. Unfortunately not all of us are regularly acquainted with those who could potentially be our most valuable connections. Not all of us have the world's most solid connections in our families or circle of friends. Now you can just accept this fate or you can change it. Simple as that. And the easiest way to change such a fate is show someone what you have for no charge.

If volunteering is nothing more to you than "working for free," you, friend, are a short sighted individual. And you are missing out on opportunities someone more ambitious (and far sighted) than you will steal from you.

How many times have you heard desperately unemployed people gabbing, "If only someone would give me a chance, I would make it worth their while," or "If only I could get my foot in the door somewhere, anywhere, I would go far." Here's a better idea. Instead of sitting on your ass waiting for someone to give you a chance, why don't you give yourself a chance? All that time you waste whining and complaining could be used more productively volunteering somewhere for someone who could be a potential employer or connection, possibly both. Trust me, the people interviewing you read and hear the same news you do. They know the economy is in hell. But they don't care. They only care about why *you* have been out of work for the past ten months. And you had damn well better come with something better than "the economy sucks" or "nobody's hiring" or "I have been job *hunting* for the past ten months." Put yourself in Human Resources' shoes. Who would you hire: someone who things seem to happen to or someone who makes things happen?

Networking Journey

When I was in college, I heard the word *networking* a lot. It wasn't until after college that I realized I didn't even know what networking really meant. I used to think networking consisted of going to an event, like a luncheon or a career fair, and listening to speeches or watching presentations, followed by meeting people, chatting with them, and collecting business cards. I thought that these events would make getting a job very easy. One of my worst networking experiences happened a few months after college. For an organization of which I was a member, I volunteered to work in one of the booths, which helped me get into this almost-thousand-dollar event for free. After completing my duties, I took advantage of the chance to collect over a hundred business cards, the vast majority of which were from people I never even met. I didn't care. To me, this was a chance to spam my resume out to a whole bunch of people, a few of whom would have to offer me something. Right? Wrong!

True networking involves a give-and-take relationship. All parties involved must feel they can benefit from doing business with the parties they have interacted with. Whether you are talking about getting a job or starting or growing a business, the people you are dealing with must be convinced you have something to offer that is of value to them. Offering a taste, a free sample, a "try before you buy" will put more people at ease and in a state of mind where they will at least try you. Remember, as long as you are unemployed or starting a business that is going nowhere right now, what you need more than anything right now is to give someone a chance to experience what you have to offer. And in a world full of people who feel like they must get paid now "lest they die tomorrow," it is a breath of fresh air when someone is willing to let someone else try something for free.

Work Now, Get Paid Later

Look here, I'm going to break it down to you like this: as long as you are not getting hired anywhere to do work you are getting paid for now, you may as well start doing some work someone may pay you for later. Because doing volunteer work is far more valuable than updating your resume. For you and for whomever you are volunteering. You are not only showing someone right now what you have to offer, but you are getting to know people now who potentially will have immeasurable value to you later. Work you do as a volunteer now is work you could get paid someday to do. But no one will pay you to be a job interviewee.

And to you new, unknown music bands out there who are on the streets peddling your CDs for a measly $5 or $10 bucks, why don't you try handing those babies out for free? I'll bet your CD will find its way into more hands, and that increases the chances your CD will land in the hands of someone who can be very valuable to you. Like that guy whose brother has a friend who works for a major record label that, coincidentally, is looking for fresh new flavor! I don't want to be the one to try to influence you one way or the other, but if it were my band, and we have been working our asses off in her basement or his garage for the past two years with only the occasional small-time gig as thanks for our efforts, I would much rather check my voice mail to find a message from that record company guy who wants to give us a break than to count the fives and tens we made on the street today!

Just A Taste

Becoming a volunteer is an investment, transforming possibilities into opportunities. The reason people may be reluctant to try a product or service you're offering is because they don't need it. More likely, though, they won't try you they don't know you. But then you may ask, "Well then, how will they get to know me if they won't try me?" That is not a question for *them* to answer. That is a question for *you* to answer.

You must figure a way around the barrier that stands between you and the opportunity you see right in front of you. Experience proves time and time again that nothing will get people to give you a chance quite like letting them try a little for free. You see, when you are not afraid to offer a little for free, the confidence you have in your product of service shines through. People can see that you are motivated by more than mere monetary gain. They are more prepared to believe you have something to offer that they care about. And by "they" I mean prospective employers as well as prospective customers.

When you allow prospectives to "taste" (figuratively or literally) a sample of your products or services, they will remember the taste you gave them later on when the time comes to decide whether to invest in you. But if you need to get paid now, they will take one look at you, make a value judgment, and decide yes or no. Does the latter sound like opportunity to you? And yes, that goes for job interviews like anything else. Sometimes your prospective employer will have decided whether or not to hire you with one look, before you even open your mouth. More often than that, they have decided once your resume has arrived, before they've ever seen you. If that fits the profile of the kind of opportunity you want to pursue in this world, go right ahead. But I assure you, countless other people are finding opportunity far easier, faster, and less painfully.

Invest Today in Tomorrow's Fortune

What you'll discover during your volunteering experience is while you are helping out others, you are helping yourself as well, perhaps even more.

I'm not going to try to candy-coat the idea of volunteering. Volunteering is going to cost you time and even money (if nothing else, at least transportation expenses). But what you stand to gain from the experience of volunteering cannot be measured in terms of cost.

I have known far too many people who have found jobs and even careers through volunteering to doubt its immeasurable value. Volunteering offers you a golden opportunity to find direction in your life. Sure, you can sit in some danky career counselor's office, have them observe you and document your traits and personalities in order to use that information to match you with careers that supposedly best suit your disposition, character, and personality. Or you can find your vocation the old-fashioned, true-and-true way: discipline and practice. And there is no quicker way to get to work on that than by volunteering.

While some of us were in college doling out tens (or hundreds) of thousands of dollars while rolling around in uncertainty as to what we wanted to get our degree in (because, seriously, how many people know what they want to do with the rest of their lives at age 18?) a handful of our peers took a far wiser path and decided to do volunteer work or got a job or joined the military. While we were in college spending ungodly tuition – studying what we were *maybe* interested in, learning how to not have a clue what's going on in the real world – our peers were trying this and trying that for free.

Volunteers may not get paid for their work, but moving from one volunteer job to another sure is far less expensive – and, I might add, far more valuable – than moving from one college major to another. People who get out into the real world to try different jobs, roles, and functions have a far better idea what they want to major in than the vast number of us who go into college fresh out of high school.

I would also like to add that in addition to the lack of real world experience offered by many college programs, the number of junk majors is increasing every year. In case you don't know what I mean by "junk majors," I'm referring to those subject areas of concentration that are all but nonsensical, without even the semblance of anything designed to help anyone get a job. Why in the hell would you spend all that tuition money to study what is fun to learn in the classroom, but is all but meaningless once you graduate? If you want to study something that's fun to learn, there are places and ways far less expensive than college!

Of course, some such majors may be valuable to those who want to be lifelong scholars. But most of them are junk to those who want to use their major to help them start a job or career.

Courses at good colleges should be commended for their complexity, as well as the fact they teach you how to think on a much higher level. But that's not the same as saying that colleges and universities are good at getting students employed after graduation. And if you take a good look at how much the tuition of the average college charges for just one semester, you had damn well better demand they help you get employed somewhere after graduation!

Volunteering Vs. Schooling

Sorry, I just couldn't resist. I needed to have a chapter devoted specifically to college students. So if you're not a college student, feel free to skip this chapter.

Ah, the wonders of college tuition. Tuition and fees. Room and board. Books. Good God! Is there any end to what college students have to pay for? I sure hope your mama or rich uncle was able to take care of your college costs. Because if you borrowed your way through college, you had better believe your blood is going to pay that money back!

And then there is the studying. No one can deny that your major will dictate how much time and energy you will need to devote to studying. Well, that and your capacity to take on such a major. Thank God some majors put you on the career track right away. Such majors are actually designed to prepare you to work in the field you are studying. Unfortunately the harsh reality, whether you want to accept it or not, is that too many majors are full of pork. Too many college students find themselves highly enthusiastic about majoring in a field of study only to find the study worthless to them after graduation. Other college students figure it doesn't matter what they major in as long as they get that bachelor's degree.

So what am I saying? Am I suggesting you drop out of college as quickly as possible? Absolutely not. I am suggesting that as soon as possible you start doing volunteer work somewhere off campus. Start by volunteering in the field you chose as your major. Find out as quickly as possible: 1) if this is truly the field and/or area of concentration you wish to stick with, 2) as much as you can about the job market for this field, and 3) if there are any extra courses you can take to increase your options in the field after graduation. For our purposes, volunteering is like being a good student: study, experience, inquiry.

I truly believe the volunteering experience will help you decide once and for all not only if you are majoring in a field you will love to work in, but if you should remain in college at all. College is too expensive for you to have no idea, or even merely a so-so idea, of what you want from the experience. Three to four hours of volunteering per week will prove more valuable than the credit hours of a year's worth of courses. You may develop skills and contacts that will lead to an internship or even job in the field. Some college students, because they were at the right place at the right time, had employers patiently waiting for them to acquire the degree so the employer could hire them.

I understand volunteering off campus may sound silly to you when you compare it to a work-study job that you could be getting paid for. After all, if you don't like your major, you can just change it. And when you are a broke college student, overtired from studying, doing any work for free sounds like too much to ask. But I promise three to four hours of volunteering can help you make the important decisions you need to make about your major and your future. Just give it a try.

Let Them Taste The Milk, Then Make Them Buy The Cow

Whether your ultimate goal is to get a job or start a business, or even to get a record deal for your music band, the focus right now is to allow people to sample the product or service you have to offer now. Give your prospects a pleasant experience of your products or services, and you will find yourself in a better position to ask them to pay for it someday. But the objective right now is to get your product in their hands or your service in their experience. Eliminate, or at least greatly reduce, the financial risk, and increase the numbers of people who will try you out. Offer to give what you have for free, and more people and organizations will take the risk and try out what you have. Make the people hungry for what you have to offer so they will need (not just want) more from you later. Then make them pay for it.

Sounds simple enough, but how many people have the fortitude to stick to a goal that is slow in coming to realization? To continue to invest in a venture that is sucking away time, money, and resources, and showing only occasional positive results? For better or for worse, employers are in the position of advantage. If you are like most people, employers have far more people chasing them than have chasing you. You will not gain an advantage until you decide to do what most people won't do, namely forgo getting paid for your products and services now in the name of getting the big reward later.

Remember, it's not enough for potential regular receivers of your products and services to want you. The goal is to make them *need* you. Let them taste the milk, then make them buy the cow.

Give Them a Sample Today

Nothing lowers the risk of wasting your money quite like having tried it before you brought it. Kinda like in those stores when they give you a free sample of a product to help you decide if you're going to buy that product. Now there's always a risk involved. You could find yourself volunteering for an employer that will never hire you. Your band can give free copies of your CDs to hundreds, and only have a small percentage of those people buy from you again, or attend your future gigs or concerts. But I can assure you that if you persist and put time, effort, and determination into the venture, you will come out a winner. Show people that you are willing to put sweat and heart into what you want to sell to them.

There are many reasons people guard their money nowadays, but one of the reasons is the vast number of proposals pitched daily to get money from us come from people who are not real. These daily proposals come to us in so many forms – i.e., newspaper and magazine ads, commercials, infomercials, junk snail mail, junk e-mail, street beggars, telemarketers, people supposedly associated with a nonprofit organization stupidly asking for your credit card number in the middle of the freakin' city sidewalk – because most of the vendors that approach us daily are out to get our money, not provide us with something we consider worthwhile.

If you want a potential employer or potential customer to be more receptive to what you are trying to offer than they would be to, say, a panhandler, you need to be willing to put heart in what you are offering. And nothing says "I have what you will want to buy" like letting people try a little for free. Volunteer your services, and employers will believe you really care about getting a job. Volunteer your products, and people will be more convinced you care about what you are trying to sell them.

If No One Will Give You a Job, Give Yourself One

"Yeah, but I've got ten kids to feed plus I've gotta take care of grandma. I don't have time to work for free." Okay, fine. Have it your way. But while you are making excuses, there are others who are making opportunities. As long as you are unemployed yet need a job to survive, you have time to volunteer. Here's a valuable life lesson: if you want something badly enough, you will find a way to get it.

Volunteering is cheaper and far too often more valuable than schooling. Furthermore, your experiences as a volunteer can lead you back to school to study in an area or field you may have never even considered before.

Now keep in mind there are volunteering positions that actually require previous experience, education, and/or training. But the vast majority of volunteering assignments require no previous experience, and are instead excellent places to start to gain experience. And even many of the ones that do require experience, you can likely get that experience from another volunteering position with the same employer.

Depending on who you are volunteering for, getting started as a volunteer can be much less daunting with far less paperwork than starting as an employee. In fact, some volunteer positions require almost no paperwork.

Volunteering provides an opportunity to find your vocation, your place to contribute to society, your way of giving yourself to the world.

Volunteering For Second Chances

This is not just another piece of recycled advice. Volunteering can indeed be the crucial missing component to your job hunt being a complete triumph. If you are unwilling to give volunteering a try, to whom do you suppose you can pass the blame if one job prospect after another turns out to be nothing more than the cause of disappointment and distress?

It is indescribable what a tremendously positive force volunteers are in this or any other society. People have gotten second chances because of volunteers. Silenced voices have been heard because of volunteers. Movements have been started and put into motion because of volunteers. There are people in this world who may have had no choice (or at least thought they had no choice) but to get used to and live with cruel fates had it not been for the intervention and tireless efforts of volunteers.

Earlier I mentioned that this book is not intended to make you a noble individual. But think about the advice you have read in newspapers and the Internet on being the ideal job candidate. There are many different pieces of advice for many different people. But an overwhelming majority agrees that the more confident the candidate, the more promising the prospect. And what easier way is there to have the confidence you need for that next interview than to talk to you prospective employer about an experience that made you feel good? When you converse with a potential employer about an experience listed on your resume that touched your heart, you speak more freely and with more confidence and conviction than you do with experience that merely tickled your brain. Reciting facts (i.e., "My duties on that job basically consisted of.….") and kissing the employer's ass (i.e., "I'm a people person and a wizard on a wide variety of computer applications") while making sure your breath don't stank and your hands are in the proper place at all times does nothing but produce much boredom and ample drool.

On the other hand, sharing with the employer a detailed account of something you did that made you feel proud, and others feel proud of you, flows from you so naturally, with no rehearsing. And the employer will pick up on that, and the passion behind it. Now the employer is proud of you. You helped someone get a second chance. And now you may be rewarded with a second chance.

It's amazing how much rehearsing people start doing after reading those dribbles of job interview advice. And in the end, the passion wins over doing what you were "supposed" to do.

Find Today What You Will Use Tomorrow

Magazines ads. TV commercials. Websites. Articles in the newspaper Jobs and Careers section. Even the blogosphere. There's always blah blah blah about some revolutionary new university major. Or an institute that offers training in a career that will be in huge demand five years from now. Or a new program of classes that all the cool kids have already enrolled in, and you'd better hurry up if you want to be one of the movers and shakers. At some point, you have to suppose there is a better way.

Truthfully, it's great there are so many advanced learning, higher degree, and hot career courses and programs so readily available. But stop for a few minutes to think about this. Before you get on the hot career school bandwagon, ask yourself, "What do I want from these programs?" Do you honestly believe you will have anything resembling a guarantee of employment – let along that super career garbage they keeping shoving down your throat – once you graduate from the program? First of all, you are enrolling in a program you saw on TV or the Internet, heard on the radio, or read about in a newspaper or magazine. That alone has "I'm screwed" written all over it. Why? Because if you are lucky, you are one of hundreds who are enrolling in that same program. If you are unlucky, you are one of thousands or even millions enrolling in that same program. Do you honestly believe these people don't know what they are doing? When a career is already in great demand or soon will be, educational institutions, whether nonprofit or for-profit, see huge marketing opportunity. And the industries love it because before too long, the employers in these industries will have more candidates that they need to fill their positions in every area of that profession.

So what now? You've spent all that money for schooling in a career you probably didn't want to get involved with in the first place. And now you've graduated, and you feel lied to because you don't see the huge market for the profession you just spent all that time and money to study. Truthfully, there probably really is a huge market for that profession. The reason it doesn't feel that way to you is because at least two hundred other people have their eye on the same pie you're trying to get a piece of.

Now that you've stopped to consider all of the above BEFORE enrolling in that hot new program at that highly acclaimed educational institution that promises top quality instruction and training on careers that promise to be in huge demand five years from now, you can open your eyes and see the real opportunity will be for the potential employers, not the potential employees.

Perhaps if we little people would try a different way, the accounting departments of big businesses and educational institutions would stop having so much in the debit column of their *Suckers* accounts. (Oh and by the way, accounting students, the *Suckers* account is in the "Assets" section of Big Boy Company's balance sheet.) A few weeks, perhaps a few months of volunteering is worth years of schooling. And if your volunteering experience leads you to pursue further learning, licensing, and/or certification in a certain field, at least you will have known from tried skill and practice that you want to learn more in this particular area. That's much better than the reasons most college students bounce from one major to another.

And by the way, in case you're concerned about employers getting paid while you don't, because you're a volunteer, think about this: these businesses and organizations are going to get paid off of you anyway. So the question you need to ask yourself is, "Will I help them get paid while I suffer in misery and hating my job, or will I help them get paid while I enjoy doing something I love?"

Find a Hole And Fill It

What you are trying to accomplish here is getting someone to need what you have to offer. Those who work in fields such as marketing and advertising are intimately familiar with the concept of creating and fulfilling a need. It is simply not enough for people to *want* what you have to offer. For one, your products or services may be on a list – a long list – of things others *want*, Secondly, when budgets are cut, anything that is not perceived as necessary will find itself on the wrong end of the ax. Thirdly, creating wants instead of needs will win you a lot of one-timers and very few long-termers.

Volunteers are always in demand. Employees are often laid off, but the work flow never stops or even slows down (unless the employer is soon to go out of business, and sometimes not even then). Therefore, there is always a need for someone to get some much needed work done.

Volunteers can always expeditiously fill a hole because there is never need to "fit" the volunteer "into the budget." Sometimes the holes volunteers fill are not really that big.

Volunteers may take on the smaller tasks so the full time employees can get busy with the bigger assignments. Employers save time as well as money when they bring in volunteers. And volunteers (if they are smart) study, observe, and inquire constantly while carrying out their assignments. While volunteering, you may notice full timers working in a position you'd like to work in someday. Ask them how they got the job. Ask them what you need to do to get a job like that. Maybe you need a degree or certification. Or maybe you just need someone to put in a good word for you.

Find the employer's hole and fill it. Then ask them to fill your hole. Namely, the gaping hole that stands between you and your ability to pay your monthly debts.

You Cannot Win a Game You Are Not Playing

The goal when pursuing a job or career is to get employed at the least, and to get employed in a job you'd really love at the most. It doesn't matter who is the better interviewee. Or who took more courses in college. Hell, nowadays it hardly even matters who has the most relevant education or experience. It's time to stop reading job-finding tips in periodicals and on websites, and start gaining job-finding connections. There is no advice you can read or hear anywhere that is more valuable than getting out there and meeting the people who can be your link to getting a job. There are many ways to meet such people, but for some of us there is hardly a more useful and expedient way than volunteering.

Some people would argue that they are playing the game because they have so many upcoming job interviews. By job interviews, they mean they have so many prospects, with varying degrees of promise. Just because you are called in for a job interview, that does not mean you are playing the game. I, myself, have had job interviews where the interviewer was late, didn't know my name, and never saw my resume prior to the interview. That certainly does not fit the profile of a promising prospect. That fits the profile of someone who "just wants to get this damn thing over with." You are really not in the game until you've had at least one post-interview callback. And that's just *in* the game, not winning it.

If you volunteer, on the other hand, your resume

can potentially do such magic acts as jumping ahead of the employer's five hundred other prospects. Don't underestimate the value of knowing the right people. I have seen prospects have interviews that were only formalities, not really necessary, because the person on the other side of the desk was someone with whom they were acquainted a long time before that interview.

It Is Better To Use What You Don't Have Than To Have What You Don't Use

There are so many people in this world who are getting defeated by people who are far less talented than they are. History has proven time and time again that determination will win over natural talent any day.

Determination will win over education and experience too. People who demonstrate determination and strength of will find people handing them opportunity. Because when a person is determined, you know they are going to succeed, so why not have them succeed with, or for, you?

Determined people find a way. While things are happening to everyone else, determined people make things happen. Determined people do what others describe as risky, silly, and just plain stupid. But in the end, the craziness pays off, and everyone finally understands what the determined person was trying to do. Because, of course, hindsight is 20/20. But now it's too late because the determined person has overcome and succeeded, and is now moving on to the next crazy venture the commonfolk will not comprehend. Volunteering when you really need a paid job? That's crazy! Sure it is, for the short-sighted.

Consider All Options

So you say you have done everything to get a job, and there really is no one out there who will hire you. You have made (or at least feel as though) your job hunt your full-time job. You have sent resumes to dozens upon dozens (possibly hundreds upon hundreds) of potential employers. You've sent paper resumes. You've sent online resumes. You always include a cover letter with your resume. You always readjust your resume, cover letter, and what not to fit the company and position you are interviewing for. And the few times you do get a job interview, you always dress your professional best, bring a fresh copy of your resume with you, arrive ten and even thirty minutes early for the interview, and say the "right" things during the interview. You carefully follow the guidelines and advice for job interviewing offered by Sunday newspapers and career counselors (physical and online). And you never, ever forget to send a thank-you letter after the interview. So you have done everything you could do to get a job, right? Surely it can't be your fault the economy is in hell and there seriously is no one hiring.

Sorry to be the one to break the news to you, but if you haven't even considered volunteering anywhere, you have *not* done everything. While you are wasting time repolishing your resume or on the Web doling out your resumes as though they were a bunch of free sammiches, you could be making connections while proving yourself to someone via volunteer work.

One of the reasons many of us do not find the great

opportunities we supposedly see the rest of the world enjoying is because of the crap we waste out time doing. Volunteering takes up far less time than some of the things we waste our time on, yet few people recognize its value. And we wonder why so many people think of us as a greedy, selfish nation. Most volunteer opportunities ask for three to four hours a week from you. By giving three to four hours a week of your time, you can gain that which people up from dawn to dusk tuning resumes and tweaking cover letters, with the occasional job interview in between, will never find.

You know, it's quite amazing. Many folks spend a whole lot of time and energy trying to impress employers to get jobs they end up hating. If that's not a waste of your life, I don't know what is.

Discover And Learn While You Are Looking

The best part about giving is that you always get back more than you give. Volunteering provides the rare opportunity to find your vocation, and yourself, while helping someone else out. What you are after is the volunteering experience. This goes beyond just the volunteering assignment. It is about the people you are meeting and helping out. It's about the work you are doing as a volunteer, and what you are discovering about yourself in the process (i.e., "Do I like this work?" "Do I want to study in this field?" "What profession would I like to learn, and in what capacity do I want to practice it?"). It's about how intimately you can get to know those who will continue to be valuable to you long after you are done volunteering in this particular department of the establishment.

In college, you can learn much about professions but very little about the real world practice of those professions.

"But what about internships and such? Isn't that a valuable way for colleges to help people learn the real world practice in that field?" Sure it is, if you are one of the lucky few who get that golden internship. But most students will get a so-so internship at best, and no internship at worst. The best internships are usually offered to those who have been systematically agreed to be the best students. What if you are not one of the "elite"? In terms of depth and scope, volunteering will usually beat the hell out of just about any internship.

Besides, while you are sitting around waiting for that golden internship, you could have already started volunteering somewhere. Who knows, volunteering may lead you directly to the sweetest internship!

Open Minds Breed Vast Opportunity

One of the main reasons some people go through life feeling like opportunity is available to everyone but them is because their eyes are wide open when someone else takes advantage of an opportunity, but somehow they go blind when opportunity comes to them. Who knows, someday you may actually be confronted with an opportunity that has the semblance of someone knocking on your door to assure you that you've just won a million dollars for your birthday. But most of life's grand opportunities first present themselves as just another happening on an ordinary day. For many grand opportunities, there will some time, and possibly hard work and sweat, before you will plainly see the glitter and starlight that was always there.

Only visionaries can see opportunity in what first appears as little more than a big headache. You must have an open mind if you are going to see opportunity in the many paths available to travel. Many of the best paths don't look very attractive when you first see them. But a visionary can see into the future. A visionary can see beyond the dirt, the filth, the grime. A visionary can see gold where most people see crap.

It's incredible how so many people in this world miss out on life's good fortunes not because the good fortune never comes to them, but because their minds are not open enough to see the good fortune when it comes. Good fortune, like many other things in life, wears many disguises. One disguise of good fortune is everydayness. Many of life's treasures, at first glance, hardly look distinguishable from the everyday junk. But every pile of trash has a treasure within it. Some people can see it, and some cannot.

Volunteering looks and feels to many like working for someone for free. But people with open minds and large visions see much reward in volunteering. And when I say "reward" I'm not just talking about "that great feeling inside" of knowing you helped someone out, or knowing you did a good deed today. I mean, sure, these people do indeed get that great feeling inside. But they get much more than that. Volunteers meet people who can be connections or contacts for them to use in the future. You could meet someone who can someday help you grow a business, or you may meet someone who will offer you a seriously reduced price plumbing job.

I'll tell you what, though. You are only going to receive what you are open minded enough to receive. It has often been said that "No one is going to hand you anything in this world." That is a slab of crap. There are people in this world who will hand you something. You just have to know where to find them. Then you have to convince them it's worth their while.

Let Them Know How Committed You Are

We live in a society where people feel entitled to get paid big and quickly for work they have hardly put any effort and no passion into. People who are willing to devote time and energy to perform tasks that benefit others, yet don't need their million dollars up front, are going to get swooped up with the quickness. Demonstrate more interest in doing something that you will feel good about and you will find people lining up to employ your services. Commitment and passion are more important to potential employers that knowledge, skills, and even experience.

How about this for a weapon in the job interview arsenal: "They loved how well I did this job when I wasn't getting paid. Imagine how much more they'll love my work when I get paid!" Dazzle them with your dedication. Remember, there are countless numbers of people who would not consider being a volunteer. Being willing to "do it for free" will help you stand out. Not to mention volunteering keeps that hole out of your resume. You may not be able to help the fact that no one is hiring right now, but you can help that you went months doing nothing constructive because of it. Volunteer work, even if it is not in your chosen field, looks better to a potential employer than a gap of many months on your resume. A huge gap on your resume looks like laziness, not stubborn effort.

Stop Waiting for a Break, And Give Yourself One

You could keep doing the same old crap, hoping to God someone will give you a break. You may have heard the famous quote, "The definition of insanity is doing the same thing over and over and expecting different results." When job interview after job interview, though you get better with each one, leaves you unemployed and frustrated, the answer is not more job interviews. Stop listening to people who tell you crap like "you need to get as many interviews as possible to land that great opportunity." No you don't. There is always another way. What you need to do is find it.

Volunteering is an excellent alternative. Showing people your stuff while gaining experience and practice time. Practice is far healthier and far less frustrating than job interviewing. While you are wasting time learning the latest techniques, tricks, and tips for being the perfect candidate, somebody else is getting paid doing a job that you would love and appreciate more than they do.

I'm going to let you in on a little secret: with the occasional rare exception, the only people who are ready to give you a break are people who feel they are going to get a break in return. Before the vast majority employs your services, they are all but absolutely certain that your services will be worth far more to them than what they are paying for the services. Someone who has gotten a sample of what you have to offer is in a far better position to make an intelligent decision about whether to give you that break than someone who has never known you beyond your resume and oral blubbery.

Don't Knock It Until You've Tried It

Many would suppose that job hunting can be, in and of itself, a full-time job. To my mind, that is ridiculous. However desperately unemployed you may be, job *searching* should never be treated as a full-time job. Volunteering would make a far more productive, and more valuable, full-time job than job-hunting.

So you wish to alleviate the job finding problem and increase your job prospects? Fancy this plan: "door-to-door" job hunting. Basically, this venture would consist of: 1) waking up bright and early, like 5 or 6am, as if to get ready to go to work; 2) dressing well and making yourself appropriately presentable to prospective employers; 3) approaching several different company offices and introducing yourself to as many people in each company as possible; and 4) leaving a copy of your resume while picking up at least one business card. Sounds okay in theory, but in practice?

Folks, I'm not going to deny I am preaching here, specifically about the *power* of volunteering. Investing some of your time, giving a piece of yourself to someone for the promise of something far greater in return. You don't have to be a seasoned investor to know that the goal of any investment is to have far greater returns than deposits. When you volunteer, you will always get more from the experience than you put into it because you will, at the very least, gain a skill and/or behind the scenes look at the employer. You know, lending a helping hand has an amazing effect on people. When you help someone, they somehow feel indebted to you. Why don't you give it a try? I will offer one guarantee: volunteering will be well worth your time and effort. But volunteering, like anything else, is what you put into it. If you perform the tasks you are asked to perform, talk to people, and ask questions, you will find opportunities you would not believe.

The Experimentation Factor

While employees on most jobs are expected to perform dutifully regardless of how drudging, dreary, or tedious the work may become, volunteers are free to move around and experiment with different kinds of duties and experiences. Volunteers should always move on before the work reaches the point of being dull and boring. A volunteer is someone who helps others while increasing him/herself. Employees, on the other hand, are expected to *do* their job, not *like* their job.

One could argue convincingly that the volunteer stands to gain more than the establishment the volunteer is giving his/her time to. Volunteers can utilize skills while picking up new ones. They can move around to different roles and positions more quickly and easily than employees can. Volunteers can hop from one department to another while acquiring, using, and developing all kinds of new skills. Not to mention how developing new skills potentially opens up a whole new world. You might start thinking of going back to school to study subjects you may not have given a second thought to before. You may look for jobs in fields that you previously wouldn't have touched with a ten foot pole. Volunteering is just about the loudest and clearest example of how helping someone else out directly is really helping yourself out indirectly. Donating time is more rewarding than donating money. You are not involved with the party to whom you are donating money. But you always know who and what you are giving your time to. Volunteering is noble because it involves giving of oneself. In a world where everyone wants to get paid right now, a volunteer stands out among the crowd. The rewards of becoming a volunteer don't come as fast, but when they do rain, they pour.

The Gratefulness Factor

"The successful networkers I know, the ones receiving tons of referrals and feeling truly happy about themselves, continually put the other person's needs ahead of their own." –Bob Burg

The best way to get what you need is to give others what they need. You will find that when you lend a helping hand to others, you will soon have people lining up to help you when you are in need. People are inspired when they see others lending an unselfish helping hand, especially in this day and age. They may not talk about it, but rest assured they feel the inspiration. It's human nature to feel compelled to help those who unselfishly help others.

The helping hand of volunteers, especially enthusiastic volunteers, sure has a way of making the normal course of events far less daunting for the full-time employees. Sometimes just having a volunteer to take care of the smaller tasks so full-timers can focus on the bigger duties is worthy enough of thanks.

There is no denying that volunteers receive more thorough praise and immediate gratification than employees. And if you are an employee whose job is made a little easier because of the volunteers who come in to lend a hand, you can feel the burden being lifted when the volunteer comes in. At the hospital, I didn't realize how helpful I was as a volunteer until I started working full time. When an enthusiastic volunteer comes in to be that extra hand of help, you can't help being grateful to them. Something inside you makes you say "thank-you." Strange, you don't quite feel such an obligation as often when co-workers lend a hand. Perhaps it's because while you're thankful, you also know that's the co-worker's job and they are getting paid to help.

Another measure of "thank-you" I always liked to give the volunteers who helped out is answering whatever questions they had about the hospital. And if they wanted to work there, I would give them advice on how to proceed and what to expect. This is a tiny sample of the kind of helpful, sometimes inside, information you need to increase your chances of having more fruitful job interviews. Yet it's incredible how many people would prefer those trifling job interviews with people they don't know, and a potential employer they've never heard of!

After a mere eight months of volunteering for the hospital, I knew more about the hospital than some employees did. By the time human resources interviewed me for the full-time job, I dare say I had more ammunition than most of my competition because I knew my way around the hospital, and I knew what was expected of me in the position I was interviewing for because of what I had seen, observed, and experienced, not from the babbles of some lame, vague job description. And I already knew the people who would be my coworkers and superiors. After human resources, I had an interview with a manager who already knew me and seen me in action. What did I need to tell him? The man already knew my work ethic. All he needed to see was my resume. Quite frankly, just between you and me, I don't think he gave a damn about my resume.

Find/Discover You Strengths/Passions

Volunteers get all the breaks because they are willing to do what many others are not. Everyone has something valuable to offer – whether or not they take the time and energy to tap into it and develop it – but not everyone is willing to offer what they have for free. Whether you want to get a job, start a business, propel your music band, or find any other kind of success, you have not tried everything if you have not tried offering your products and/or services to anyone for free. Sure, we'd all like to get paid, and right now, for whatever we give to others, whether individuals or businesses or other establishments. But the reality is that we are living in the Information Age, where people are getting more messages constantly than they could possibly know what to do with. And today, more than ever before, everyone is claiming to be the best prospective recipient of the investment of your dollar. So who do you believe? Who do you try out? Well, there are many factors to consider. But I have no doubt that those who are willing to allow others to try their products and services for no charge are going to be the first most people will be willing to sample.

Volunteer Etiquette

Yes, there is an etiquette to volunteering. Your services are valuable to, and much appreciated by, many organizations. But valuable does not mean irreplaceable. Some employers mention – but all employers expect –their volunteers exhibit professionalism expected from full-time employees. Volunteers have as much a need to put on their best face as any employee. And don't forget how this especially holds true for your purposes because you are trying to convince someone to employ you.

Here are some guidelines to carry with you through your volunteering experience:

1. Show up on time.

Establishments employ the services of volunteers for the same reason they employ the services of paid workers, because they have work that needs to get done effectively and efficiently. You must be both reliable and dependable if you are going to offer your volunteer services to anyone. Whether you are a paid worker or a volunteer, you are wasting the employer's time with tardiness, last-minute call-offs, and not showing up. And for them, time is money. You may not be a paid employee, but if you agree to a shift or time slot to work, you are honor-bound to come through. And if you don't, the employer will dispense of your services and give the job to a more reliable volunteer or paid employee.

2. Wear what you were told to wear and do the job you came to do.

The establishment that employed your volunteer services did so because they needed someone to help them out in the area you are volunteering in. If you do not dress the way you were asked to dress and/or are not doing what you were asked to do, you are not a volunteer, you are a time waster. It's best to get to work or leave.

3. Respect those who employed your volunteering services.

Obey the rules of the employer you are volunteering for. Because volunteers are not paid by the establishments that employ them, the risk with volunteers is reduced. But not eliminated. Volunteers can still harm an employer's image. While you are on the grounds of the establishment you are volunteering for, you should respect their rules, policies, and procedures. Furthermore, don't try to sell your junk on their premises. Not only is that disrespectful to the employer, but it is harassing to fellow volunteers, employees, and customers. If you have something to sell, hand potentials your business card and ask them to contact you later.

Volunteering Versus Higher Education

Countless numbers of college students spend their higher education years drifting seemingly endlessly from one major to another. And many of them will probably still end up graduating with a major that is in a subject area not true to their hearts. Now I don't know about you, but to me there is something about that whole thing that just plain sucks. Are college and university advisors and counselors not doing their jobs very well? Or is it the system designed to disable students from finding their vocation, and instead bounce from major to major? Whatever is going on, these institutions of higher education are not adequately preparing students for the real world that is dangerously close ahead of them. These institutions of higher education are putting students on a raft and dragging them to the middle of the ocean. But instead of providing paddles, life jackets, and thorough instruction with practice on how to raft their way through the waves, these institutions of higher education are throwing their students books on the *theory* of rafting and the *concepts* of the ocean, and leading students to believe that if they do their required reading and homework assignments and pass exams, they will be expert rafters. And when the students leave college – with or without a degree – they are overwhelmed by this wave, known as the real world, coming right at them!

For college students, volunteering provides an excellent opportunity to gain exposure to the real world. Forget about waiting for that exciting internship you may or may not get. Start volunteering in freshman year. Who knows, your experience may help you discover something that will change your major immediately!

Be Ambitious and Seize Opportunity Whenever Possible

Never lose sight of your goals and purposes for volunteering. Volunteering is a chance to explore and learn new things. If you see an opportunity to try something different, such as volunteering for a special event or an opportunity in a different department, seize it. Don't forget your top two objectives/priorities: 1) getting potential employers to see you in action, and 2) meeting people and making connections. Remember, you are giving them the help they need, so make sure you are getting what you need.

Furthermore, what employers find attractive in their employees is hardly separable from what they find attractive in their volunteers. Many employers don't expect much from volunteers, so why don't you dazzle them with your ambition? Ask questions. Make inquiries. Learn to care about the employer. Perhaps someone (hopefully someone with power and influence) will pick up on you demonstrated ambition and help work something out with you that will be beneficial to you and the employer.

Orientation to the Big, Bad City

I have no doubt the tourist bureaus (or whatever the city department in charge of cashing in on sucker tourists is called) of these big cities are practically kicking their feet up in the chairs and waiting for the money to come flooding in, out of the arriving buckets. Forget *having* attractions; big cities *are* attractions in and of themselves. And many big cities have all kinds of tourist rides, sites, attractions, and events to guide tourists through the city. And please let us not forget the souvenirs!

Why not try volunteering? Volunteering is a great way to gain orientation to the big, unfamiliar city. Or, heck, even the smaller unfamiliar city. You can meet people and make friends while helping out an organization or institution. If you play your cards right, someone may even offer to give you the free tour. And all this while making connections that could land you a job or business opportunity in the new city. You see why it pays to be open-minded? This is yet another example of how open-minded people create opportunities for themselves where their more closed-minded counterparts see none.

I was born and raised in Chicago. And I have visited other major cities, some at which I was fortunate enough to have a friend who was able to give me a personal tour. I can tell you from personal experience that tourists are too often duped simply because they don't know any better. The tourists don't know this new city – or anyone in it – so they don't realize there may be better, far less expensive orientations to the new city. And when you live downtown, you see on a daily basis how much your city overcharges tourists to get to know only a tiny portion of this metropolis! Whenever I hear a friend of mine who's not from Chicago is one his/her way, I do whatever possible to keep them as far away from Touristville as I can. Touristville is truly the most expensive neighborhood in any big city!

Volunteering Value

As if volunteering did not have enough pluses already, volunteering is always in demand. There is nothing the economy can do to eliminate or even lower the demand for volunteers. The economy can go up, down, sideways, inside-out, it doesn't matter. Volunteers will always be in heavy demand. And while there are volunteering assignments and positions that do have educational and experience requirements, the vast majority do not. Furthermore, for the vast majority of volunteer positions that do require certain knowledge and skills, there is a training program. And boy would that be a treat. I mean, volunteering in and of itself gives you experience, but a volunteering position that gives you education as well? That's definitely something to appreciate!

You never can be too sure who you'll meet, mingle with, or work with as a volunteer. You can potentially meet new friends, new lovers, business contacts, business partners, potential customers, possible employers, or hell, even future employees. Volunteering can provide an environment of free exchange. Oh sure, networking events such as meetings, banquets, dinners, and brunches held by social clubs and professional organizations are fine. But, with the occasional exception *some* of these organizations offer, you have to pay a hefty price to get into these events. Then you are bored to death with speeches. You watch people you don't know and don't care about receiving awards and recognitions. Then you try to stifle your slobber as you are bored with more speeches. When all the madness is over, you may actually be able to meet and chat with a few of these people while you and they are wringing out your butts and shaking out your legs, which were deadened from sitting in those seats for what felt like forever. And what do you get? If you're lucky, you get a chat and a business card. If you're luckier than that, one or both of you (that is, you and your contact) actually make an effort to follow up.

Volunteers demonstrate what they can offer. Volunteers offer more than speculation. You cannot possibly know what someone can offer you if all you did was share a brunch table with them and talk about business. True networking is not an exchange of business cards. True networking is an exchange of business. Quid pro quo. Something I want for something you want. Something I have for something you have.

We have all seen, heard, and read advertisements where someone claims to offer something incredibly amazing, and then claim there is no catch to it. (So obviously these people are motivated not by personal profit, but by social conscience, right?) Personally, what I find incredibly amazing is how condescending such ads are to their audiences. Are you really supposed to be stupid enough to believe that these people are going to offer you the world and ask almost nothing in return? You don't have to patronize perspective employers, customers, clients, or fans like that in order to find some success in your life. You can show, rather than tell, people the truth. And you will win much respect and much more admiration in return for your troubles. Of course, I hope you don't have to go way outside of yourself to be capable of giving yourself to others.

If you are truly offering quality products and services, you should have no qualms about letting someone sample them for free. When we say quality, we are talking about what is valued by the receiver, not the provider, of the products and services. Anyone can toot his own horn, claiming that what he has is the best you'll ever get, and how lucky you are to have met him or saw his commercial.

It is not hard to volunteer your services when you are operating with motives more profound than greed and personal gain. Want personal gain? Okay. Driven solely by the pursuit of personal gain? Not okay.

The Volunteering Experience

Your volunteering experience can become your own personal adventure story. There are endless opportunities to do exciting things, meet interesting people, and have a learning experience unlike any other. Test the waters and see what you can enjoy. Let the experience lead you to where you'll ultimately want to be. Hey, why not just give it a try? What do you have to lose?

Think of all the ammunition you will have for your next prospective job interview. What you are doing as a volunteer does not need to be directly related to the job you are currently interviewing for. Remember, volunteering is not just about the work, the duties you perform as a volunteer. We're talking about the volunteering experience. More important that what you are doing is who you are becoming. What is your volunteering experience teaching you about customer service? Addressing customer wants? Meeting customer needs? Driving customer demand? You may be surprised how the little things you do can change a customer's who perspective about their own experience with the employer.

And how do you enhance the volunteering experience? Curiosity. For your purposes, you need to be someone who is willing to explore opportunity and try different things. Volunteer for different projects. Move on to different departments. Once you've learned all there is to learn in one volunteer position, move to another. Remember, employees may have to endure the monotony of the everyday, but volunteers don't. Anytime a volunteer does not feel he or she is growing and learning, it's time for that volunteer to move on. The volunteering experience is supposed to enrich you, not bore you.

Curiosity is an excellent way to enter many fields of endeavor. Be curious and suppose you will try different things, and you will surely have a rich and fulfilling volunteering experience. Then you will be more sure of what field and specialty you what to be hired in. Don't forget that finding out what field you'd most enjoy working in is a huge chunk of the purpose of this volunteering experience. The practice and climate will tell the story of where and how you'd fit best and be happiest as an employee. But don't just explore opportunity, experience opportunity. Have opportunity.

The World is Overflowing With Opportunity......For Those Who See It!

While the rest of the world, in their panic, are selling, the visionaries of the world, in their ecstasy, are buying. So go ahead and see the opportunity right in front of your eyes and not even try to grab it. Chances are absolutely certain that someone more far-sighted than you will steal the opportunity from you.

In the world of opportunity, the far-sighted steal from the short sighted on a daily basis. But don't take my word for it. Look around you. Think about your friend's music band – more talented than some of the rich and famous bands you see on TV and in the magazines, going to the top in the industry – struggling to find small-time gigs. Think about that family member who just can't find work in his chosen field despite the fact he has proven time and time again he is better educated and/or more skilled than those dopes that are getting hired ahead of him. Think about that friend who you know could prove she will provide higher quality, more reliable service than most of her local competitors, if only someone would give her new business a chance.

What the people in the examples above need is something different. Something aside from the usual, the traditional, the customary resume writing and advertising techniques. They need to put their products and services in front of the people so the people can taste what they have to offer. In this day and age, you need to prove you are a *necessary* risk. And you are not going to have a chance to prove anything to anyone as long as you insist on having your million dollars up front. For our purposes here, volunteering is about giving prospects a reason to give you a chance. Give it to them for free, let them experience the delight, and make them pay to get more of the delight.

Conclusion

Throughout this book, I have tried to convince you to seek volunteering as a supplement (or as an alternative) to all the other techniques and strategies for getting people to give you a break in this world. The reality is that very few, whether individuals or establishments, will give you a chance if they don't know you. And you can multiply that grim reality when you're talking about getting an opportunity amidst an economy beaten down to the ground.

One thing I will tell you for sure is that I would not try to convince you to volunteer for success if I had not seen myself and many others succeed through volunteering. This is not some study I conducted. I don't know any researchers or analysts or social scientists. (Besides, even if I did, how the hell would I know what to do with the data they would have gathered?) I never interviewed anyone about their volunteering experiences. Most of what I know about other people's experiences in volunteering came from casual conversations. The rest I know from what I've seen with my own eyes.

Volunteering is an opportunity to develop character, purpose, and professionalism, which can make you a better employee or vendor of products and services. There is a very real, very important sense of selflessness that comes with offering your time and energy to others for free. All I'm asking is for you to let the people try you for free. After you have proven your services or products worthy in their eyes, go ahead and ask them to pay to have more. There's nothing wrong with that.

My own two eyes have seen people get the chance they were looking for while volunteering. I found opportunity, more than once, through volunteering. And I have tried to share my experience with many others who were having a hard time finding a job. Unfortunately, I have succeeded with very few that I've tried to convince. I'm hoping your mind is open enough to try volunteering, something many will not.

I don't have anything to gain or lose whichever way you go. This is not an infomercial, and I don't have a product to sell you quickly for that special low price. There is no satisfaction guaranteed or return it in 30 days. All can tell you is what I've spent this book telling you: that more people will give you a chance if you let them try you without the financial risk. I believe allowing people to try what you have to offer for free will give you a more than promising return. But that's not my decision to make. That's your decision. Remember, life is like investing: the less potential risk, the less potential reward.

Epilogue

Volunteering truly offers promise and opportunity to anyone willing to consider it and try it out. There are so many people who are not finding the break they need not because they lack a high quality product or service to offer, but because they cannot convince enough people to show enough interest to try them out. Now there are some who would say such people need to do a better job of marketing themselves. But perhaps a much better, more promising way is to allow others to sample these products and services for free. If you know what you have would be great for others and give you success and prosperity at the same time, then you should have no qualms about offering a little for free.

To encourage many people who could make a success of themselves to consider allowing volunteering to aid them on such a path, I welcome you to share volunteering experiences you have had, or any experience you have had working with volunteers. Feel free to send questions, comments, experiences, and suggestions to volunteeringforsuccess@yahoo.com. I also welcome volunteering organizations, as well as any establishment that constantly seeks volunteers, to share experiences and any suggestions to add to the "Volunteer Etiquette" chapter. If you'd like your experience mentioned in future editions of this book, please include the name of the city, time of the experience, and establishment the volunteering experience took place.